SPANISH
GUITAR MUSIC

T0061042

G. SCHIRMER, Inc.

DISTRIBUTED BY

HAL•LEONARD®
CORPORATION

7777 W. BLUEMOUND RD. P.O. BOX 13819 MILWAUKEE, WI 53213

CONTENTS

To Andrés Segovia

JOTA LEVANTINA

F. Moreno Torroba

To Andrés Segovia

CONTRADANZA

F. Moreno Torroba

SONATA IN A MINOR

Transcribed by Theodore Norman

Padre Antonio Soler

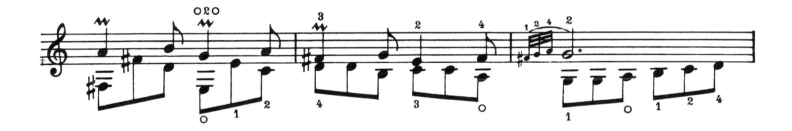

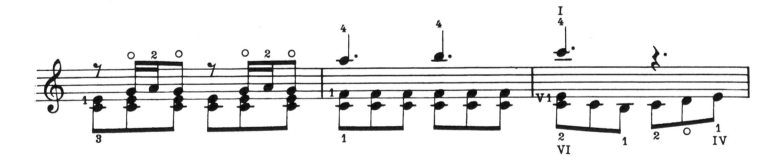

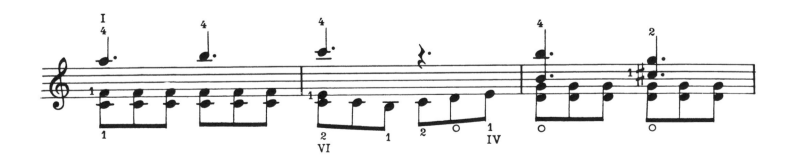

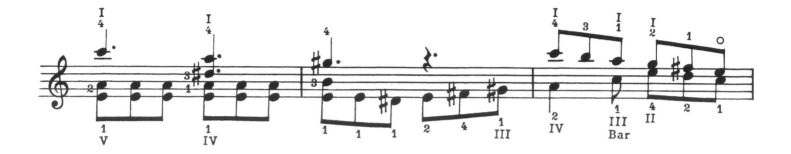

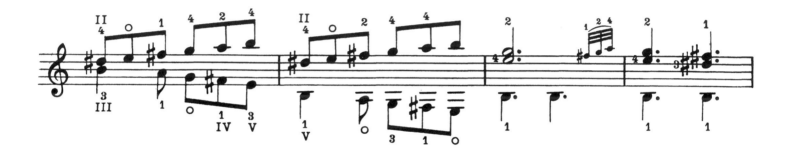

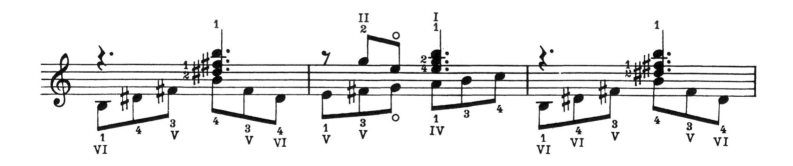

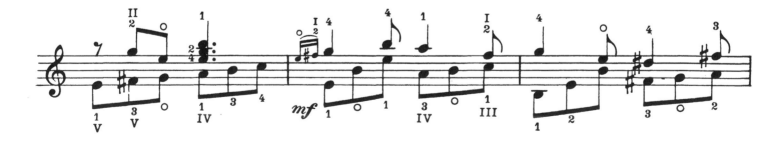

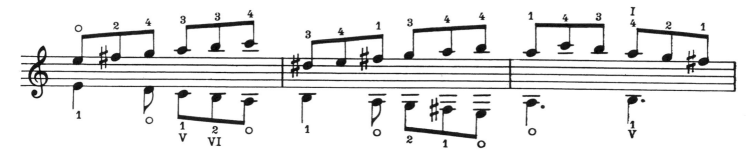

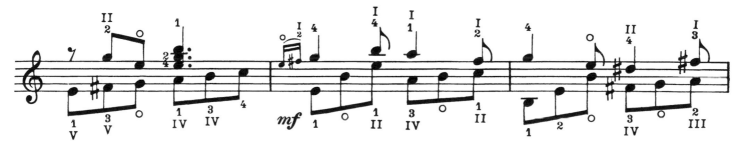

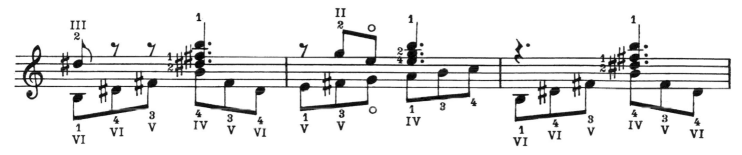

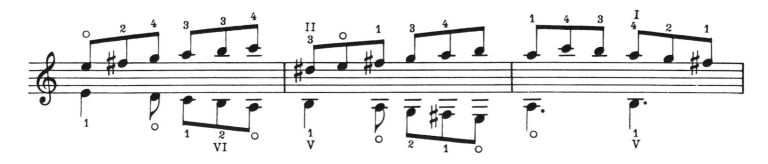

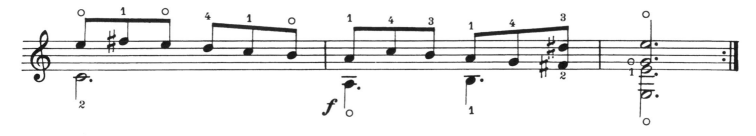

10

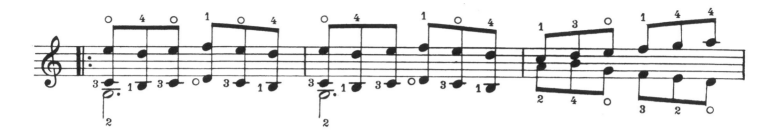

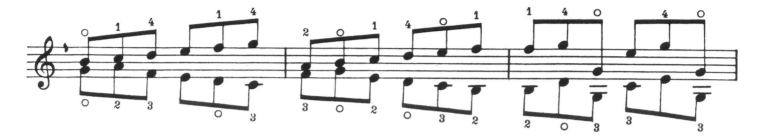

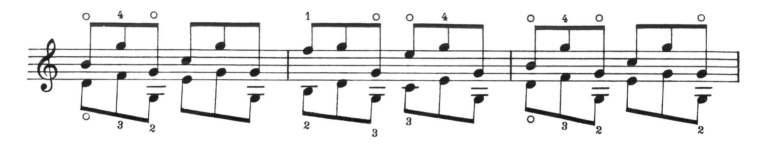

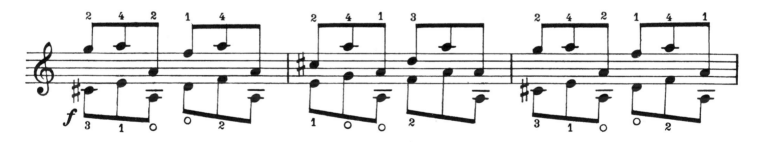

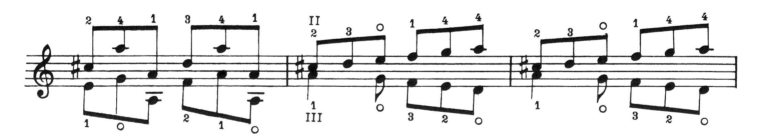

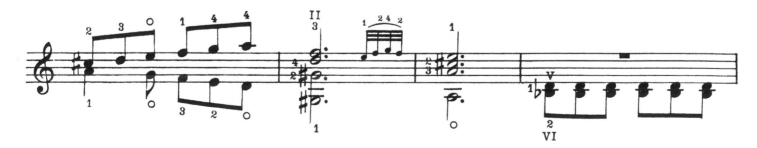

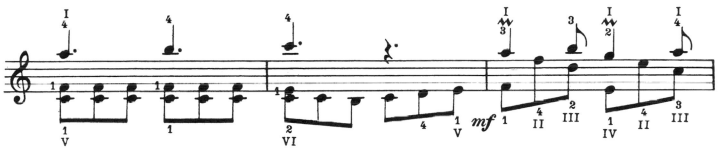

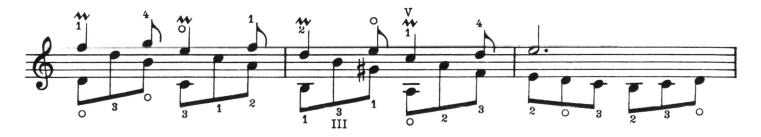

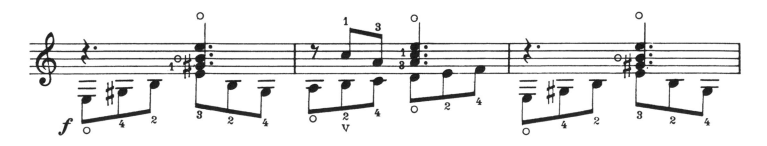

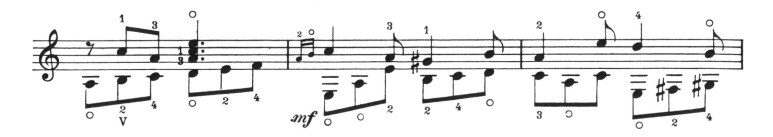

12

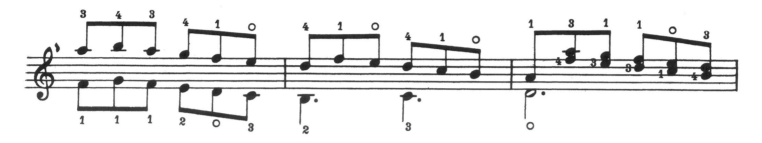

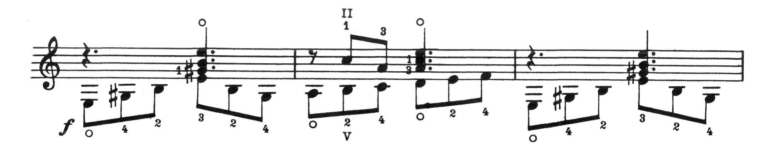

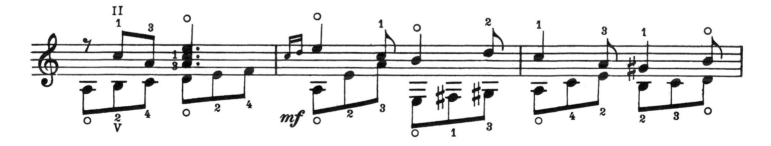

SONG OF THE FIG ORCHARD
(Cancao do figueiral)

Edited by Harold Morris

Goesto Ansunes

PETENERAS

Transcribed by Theodore Norman

Andalusian

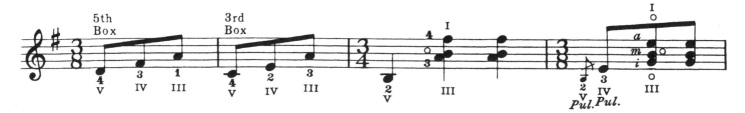

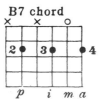

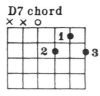

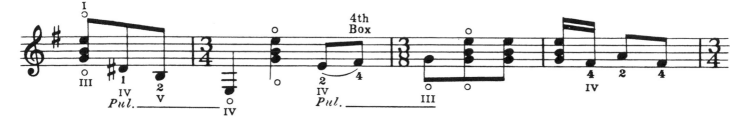

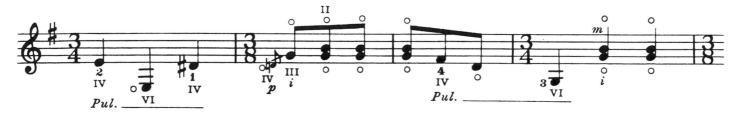

Em chord

SANDUNGA

Transcribed by Theodore Norman

Mexican

*Har. = Harmonics are produced by playing lightly above the string indicated. The finger is placed above the metal fret indicated (12th).

SONG AND DANCE
from the ballet "Chronique"

Edited by Donald Frost

Carlos Surinach

ALLEGRETTO ♩ = 60

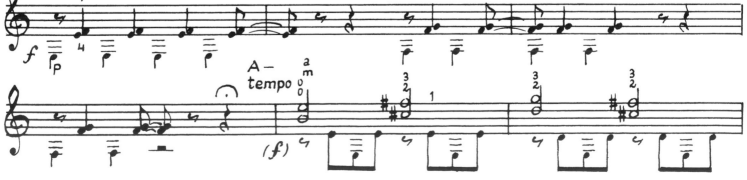

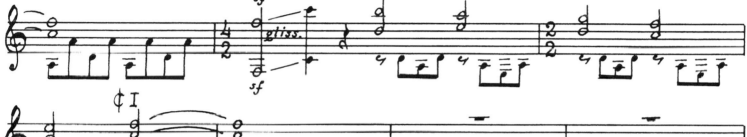

FARRUCA

Transcribed by Theodore Norman

Flamenco

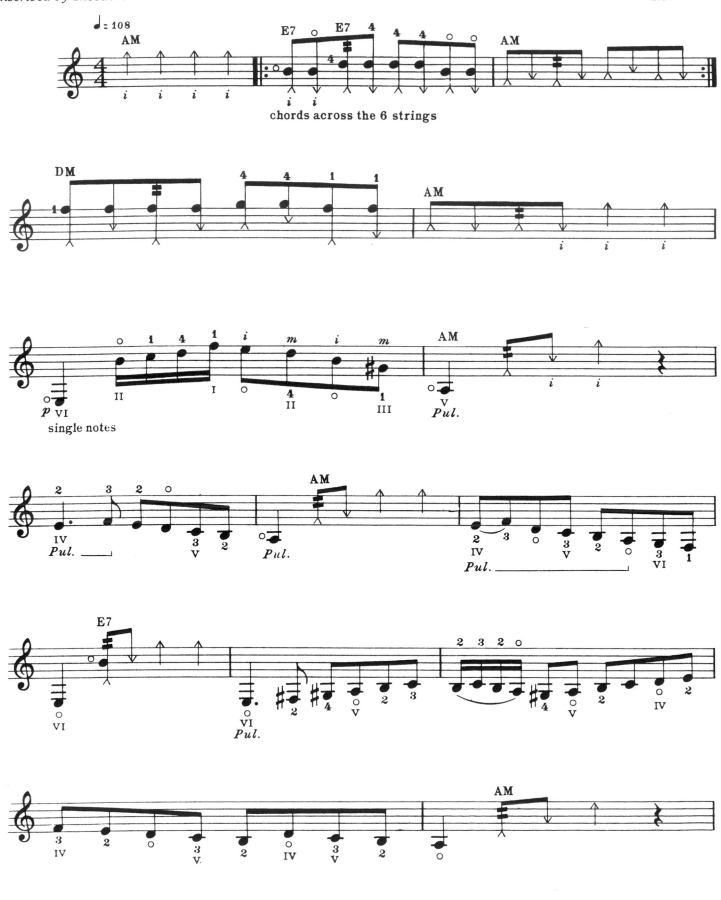

chords across the 6 strings

single notes

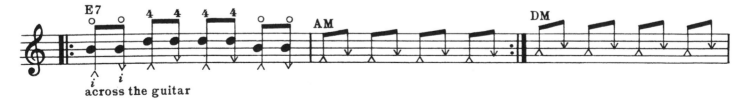

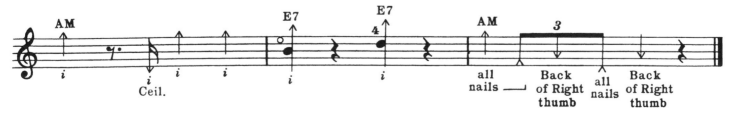

* See chord page

FLAMENCO

The notation system devised for *Farruca* includes the use of chord symbols; Am, E7, Dm *etc*.

The *rasgeado* or *roll* is notated. . .

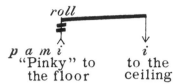

roll

p a m i   i
"Pinky" to   to the
the floor   ceiling

If the student will hold the book with the top of the page closest to the floor, the logic of the arrow notation will be apparent.

To exercise the *roll* line all the fingernails, *(i, m, a, p)* against the VIth string; then release each finger separately, starting with the *"pinky"*, a, m, i, sending each finger in rapid succession across the 6 strings of the guitar.

After the *roll* to the floor, the index finger, *(i)*, returns across the 6 strings alone to the ceiling, producing a sharply struck chord.

In the *roll* and the return of *i* to the ceiling, do not try pedantically to strike all 6 strings. Let your ear guide the resonance you think is required.

p a m i   i   The *roll* and *i* to the ceiling are *together* the equivalent of one quarter-
to the   to the   note (♩) in time value.
floor   ceiling

CHORDS IN THE FARRUCA

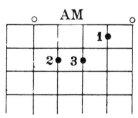

AM

with open B,
as indicated
E7

with the 4th finger down
on the IInd string
E7

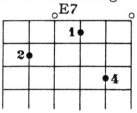

Do not sound the strings marked ×.

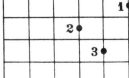

with Ist finger down,
as indicated
× × DM

with 4th finger down,
as indicated
× × DM

a m i   a   m   i
          played
Pul.   Pul.

INTERMEZZO
from the opera "Goyescas"

Version for Guitar by José de Azpiazu

Enrique Granados

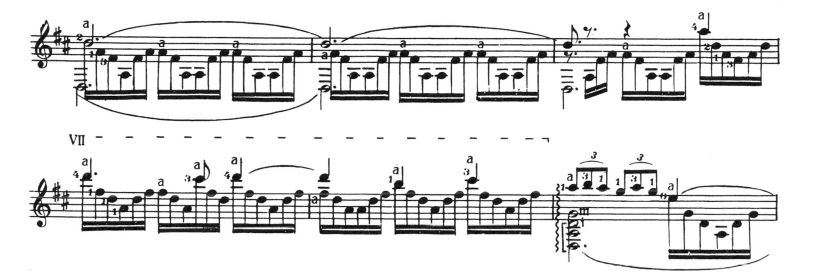

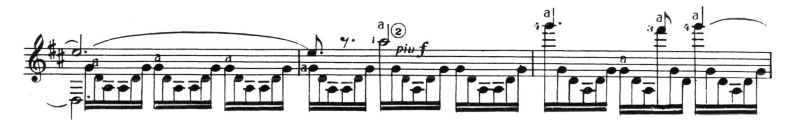

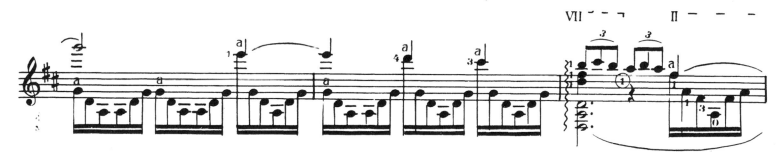

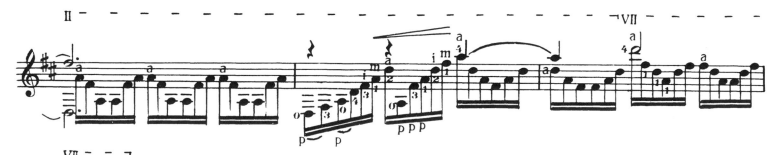

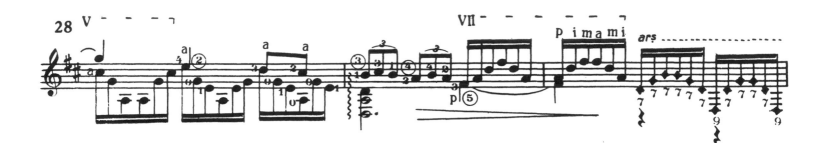

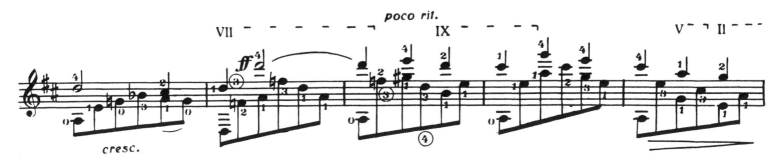

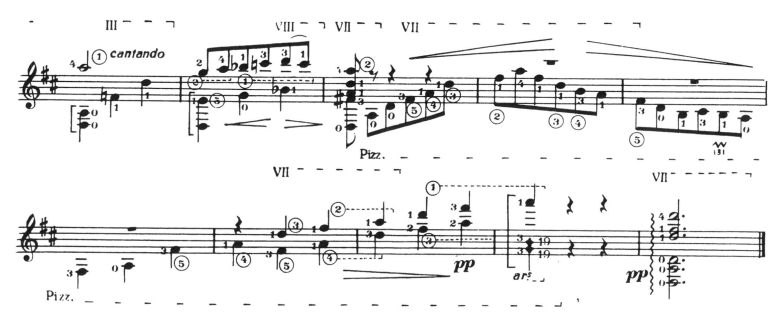